7 Easy Ways to Say NO to Almost Anyone

Stand Up for Yourself Without Looking (or Feeling) Unreasonable, Uncaring or Unkind

STEPH STERNER

Copyright © 2012 – 2018 Stephanie J Sterner

ISBN-10: 1542313740
ISBN-13: 978-1542313742

We are all responsible for the choices we make in our lives, regardless of where our ideas come from. It is always up to you what to say, how to say it and whether to say it at all. The purpose of this book is to help you to understand your options so that you can make better choices.

WANT MORE ... FOR FREE?

If you'd like to learn even more about boundaries –
like how to recognize manipulation or how to use
boundaries to improve your relationships – then head
over to **stephsterner.com**. There are blog posts,
quick tips and free downloads waiting for you.

And if you'd like something a bit more personal,
you're invited to join Steph's private Facebook group,
Boundaries and Bridges. You'll find it at
facebook.com/groups/boundariesandbridges/.
Ask questions, share your challenges and insight, get
support when you need it ... it's good to know you're
not alone!

MORE BOOKS BY STEPH STERNER

No Guilt, No Games, No Drama:
The 7 Keys to Setting Smarter Boundaries

If you're not sure when to set a boundary and when to go along, this book will get you on the right track.

(Previous title: *Set Your Boundaries Your Way: No Guilt, No Games, No Drama*)

What About Me?
The Insider's Guide to Better Boundaries

If you struggle with boundaries and you'd like to understand yourself better, this is your book. The focus is on you and the limiting beliefs, behaviors and emotional patterns that have been holding you back.

All of Steph Sterner's books are available on stephsterner.com and amazon.com.

DEDICATION

This book is dedicated to everyone who has ever been afraid to say *no*. Whether you're being manipulated or abused, or you simply feel afraid, I hope that you find the courage to break free.

ACKNOWLEDGMENTS

I'd like to thank everyone who has believed in me and supported me throughout my life. I am grateful for all the support I've received, especially from my parents and my amazing partner. I couldn't do it without you!

TABLE OF CONTENTS

PREFACE

WHAT YOU CAN EXPECT FROM THIS BOOK

Do you find yourself saying *yes* when you really mean *no*? Do you struggle to find the words that will allow you to set a perfectly reasonable boundary without feeling guilty or mean? Or do you wonder what to say when you meet with the inevitable resistance? You might dread hearing something like this:

- "I thought I could count on you. How can you be so selfish?"
- "What's more important than your family?"
- "But you're the only one I can depend on. You're not going to let me down, are you?"

If you avoid setting good boundaries because you hate arguments, you don't want to feel guilty, or you just don't know what to say, I have good news for you. *7 Easy Ways to Say NO to Almost Anyone* will give you all the information you need to change this – in less than an hour and a half.

Why so little time? Because it's not all that complicated. This book isn't about why people engage in manipulation, because understanding them isn't enough. It isn't even about why you allow people to push you around – that's a much longer book, and I want you to start making changes **now**. It's about how to deal with manipulation – or your discomfort with standing up for yourself – simply, respectfully and effectively.

With the right words, you don't need to worry about feeling mean or hurting someone's feelings. Every response I suggest is respectful. If someone is offended by it, chances are that he or she would be offended by anything other than, "Of course! I'd be glad to sacrifice my needs for yours! How soon can I start?"

You also don't need to worry about how to handle objections. The many examples in this book include objections, so you won't fall apart when someone gives you that look and says, "Why not?" You won't have to worry about how to get started, either. Each of the seven "easy ways" chapters ends with two sections. **Why isn't this easy for me?** will help you to understand what might be happening if it's hard to follow the suggestions you've just read. **Getting Started** suggests some first steps to help you get going. It's always easier once you build some momentum.

I've struggled with being a doormat. I've made my share of mistakes because I did what someone else wanted me to do – in spite of knowing that it wasn't right for me. I know how hard it can be to stand up for yourself ... and how high the price can be when you don't. That's probably why I've invested so much time and energy on this topic – researching, working with clients, giving talks and contemplating the situations I come across every day.

I decided to write this book because, whenever I gave a talk on the subject, the questions were always the same. No matter what the situation people wanted to know what to say. That's when I realized how important my particular skills were. I see what's going on behind the scenes, and I can explain it in a way that's easy to understand. And because I'm good with words, I know how to respond.

Even though it's short, this is not a one-size-fits-all book. I never suggest only one response to a given situation. I give you a number of options, along with the pros and cons of each. That way you can make your own decision, driven by your values and experience. Isn't that what you're really looking for?

No book can promise to solve all your problems. But if you're letting other people make your decisions, I can promise you this: Follow the guidelines in the book, using the words provided or choosing your own, and you will never be the same. Taking back your power – even a little of it at first – doesn't just feel great. It frees you to do the things that matter most – to live your life on your own terms.

As one reader shared:

"I found out that during all those years I should have never given in or blamed myself. All that I allowed and forced myself to do stopped that very day. Thank you Stephanie for your wonderful book, I now feel really good about myself."

And another had this to say:

"I thought I knew how to say no and always felt guilty about it - but I have found more ways to say no without hurting others feelings and getting some time and space for myself. I used to say yes, a lot, when I really didn't have the time, the expertise, the inclination, or the will to do. Don't get taken advantage of – check this book out and get your life back."

I like that: "get your life back." If you're ready to claim what's yours, then keep reading. Don't put it off – you know how easy it is to forget things, even the important ones. Each chapter in this book addresses a different aspect of difficult people and conversations. You can read them in order, or skip to the one that speaks to you the most. Approach it any way you like. Once you discover something that relates to your situation, read that section. Consider the suggested responses, and choose whatever suits you best. Then consider the possible objections and the suggestions for dealing with them. If the words offered don't work for you, choose your own. If you're nervous, practice a few times in your head – or with a friend.

Then get out there and do it. You'll be amazed at how effective a simple, respectful response can be. Those who care about you will understand your need to put yourself first once in a while. And those who don't will have to deal with the new you: someone who can no longer be intimidated by a look, a tone of voice, or an unreasonable demand. You'll quickly learn how to respond to different types of people and situations without sacrificing what matters to you: your time, your relationships, and your good feelings about yourself.

If you don't know how to say *no* when you need to, my hope is that – right now – you read this book, find something you relate to, and decide what you're going to do differently the next time someone challenges you. Because "next time" will be here before you know it!

INTRODUCTION

WHOSE LIFE DO YOU WANT TO LIVE?

The world is full of people who aren't afraid to ask for what they want ... no matter how unreasonable the request may be. They know that the world is also full of people who will give them what they ask for – and they're not hard to find.

Your brother asks you to co-sign a loan for something he doesn't need and can't afford. "It's just a formality," he says. A friend wants to start a company in your name – because his last one went bankrupt and he can't get a loan. "I'll give you a percentage of the profits – just for signing your name! This is the big one!" Your neighbor wants you to look after her youngest for the weekend because she and your daughter get along so well. But you're the one who drives the two of them everywhere. Whenever you've asked your neighbor to pitch in, she's been too busy. You were hoping to send your kids to relatives for part of the weekend just so you could catch up on your sleep.

You have the right to say *no* to these and other unreasonable requests. So why don't you?

Maybe you think that if you do this for your

neighbor, she'll be more helpful from now on. You try not to think about the fact that you're already doing all of the driving, and she's never even thanked you. You tell yourself that your brother will have the loan payment taken out of his salary, so it will be no problem. (He's not very good with money, but he wouldn't let you down … would he?) And your friend … well, you've known him since grade school. How do you say *no* to such an old friend? He's had such bad luck in business … is it really fair to stand in the way of his big chance?

What's really going on here? In our sometimes desperate need to feel good about ourselves, we make bad choices. We want others to like us, and we want to believe that we're good people. When others approve of us (as they will when we do things for them that they have no right to expect), we temporarily feel better. Guilt is replaced by a sense of relief. "I really am a good person!"

But trying to keep everyone happy just keeps you miserable. When you need someone's approval, that person has power over you. If you're going to take your life back, you'll need to let go of the idea that everyone must be (or even can be) happy. You'll need to accept some discomfort now so that you can be much more comfortable later.

Setting reasonable boundaries is good for your relationships. When you respect yourself enough to set a boundary, others respect you for it. Those who consistently try to stop you simply want what's best for **them**, even if it's at your expense. Setting boundaries allows you to see what your relationships are really based on: friendship or convenience. Do you really want to surround yourself with people who are only with you because it's convenient – because you consistently put their needs ahead of your own?

Let go of needing others to agree with your choices. Focus on what you think is best. If you're not sure, then ask yourself why. What are you unsure of: the outcome or your values?

Outcomes are never certain, and you may find that you need to become more comfortable with that. If it's your values you're unsure of, take the time to think about what really matters to you in difficult situations. Soon you'll know what you want … and you won't need anyone to tell you whether you're right.

Whose life do you want to live?

CHAPTER 1

THE FIRST EASY WAY:
BUY YOURSELF SOME TIME

Once you've committed yourself to leading **your** life instead of everyone else's, where do you begin? If you've been doing what other people want for some time, it can be difficult to start saying *no* to them. You don't know what to say, and when you do ... well, the thought of actually saying it can be a bit overwhelming. And trying to make a decision right then and there, while all the emotions are in full swing, is next to impossible. So what do you do? How do you make a good decision?

You don't. No one makes good decisions under those conditions. This is the stuff regrets are made of. So do yourself a favor: buy yourself some time.

Often we put pressure on ourselves (or succumb to the pressure of others) to make an instant decision, to know exactly what we can and cannot do without any time to think. While some decisions may be that simple ("Hey, wanna go grab a pizza?"), others are not. When the decision isn't a simple one, give yourself whatever time you need. Don't pressure yourself to make everyone else happy with a quick *yes*. And don't let anyone make you feel guilty for taking time to think. Once you commit to something, you'll find it difficult to un-commit.

It can be tough to find the words in the moment, so here are some great ways to give yourself the gift of time:

Let me see how my day goes.

I'll let you know tomorrow.

I'll check my schedule and get back to you this afternoon.

I'm not sure I feel comfortable doing that. I'll let you know in the morning.

I need to think about it. Send me an email with the details and I'll let you know.

I'm taking a friend to the airport tomorrow, so I'm not sure I'll be able to make it. Can I check my schedule and get back to you in the morning?

Co-signing a loan is more than a formality. It affects what I can borrow. Let me know the details and I'll think about it.

I'll need to give that some thought. Let's talk about it on Monday.

I feel uncomfortable agreeing to that, but I'm not sure why. Let me think about it and get back to you.

Send me your business plan and I'll think about it.

I can't even think about the weekend yet. Would you ask me again on Thursday?

If you've promised to get back to someone, remember to put it your schedule so you don't forget. The last thing you need is one more thing to feel guilty about!

Understanding Your Options

At first glance, the responses I've suggested may seem pretty much the same. But there are some important differences. Here are five things to keep in mind when you're deciding what to say:

1. **You can share why you need more time – or not. This decision is more important than you might think.**

   When you value the relationship and genuinely want to help, it's nice to give the person a reason for your hesitation. By doing so, you're reinforcing their importance to you as well as your desire to help. When you really don't want to do something, and the person asking for your time isn't close to you (and doesn't have any authority over you), I suggest avoiding reasons. Over-explaining is a way of giving away your power. It gives the other person something to argue with. This tactic can be used to wear you down, whether you're explaining your need for more time or the reason for your final decision. Don't give your power to someone who will disrespect it.

   A brief explanation may also make the other person aware of what this will cost you. Pointing out that co-signing a loan affects what you can borrow in the future serves this purpose. There is no need to delve into how much you might want to borrow or why. Keep it as simple as possible.

2. **You can (and often should) ask for more information.**

   In this case, you're doing more than just "buying time." You're letting the person know that there is more for you to consider. You'll need to know, for example, how much your brother wants to borrow – and how difficult it will be for him to make the payments. Don't be afraid to ask questions about his income and expenses. Under other circumstances, that would be private. But if he wants you to take legal responsibility for his loan, you have the right to this information. How else can you assess the risk?

In the case of the "friend" who wants to put your name on his business, requiring a business plan communicates the seriousness of such a decision. Of course, he may bring you one. But at least you've given yourself the time to consider the situation. And you'll have even more time if you choose to review the plan.

3. **You can choose whether to share how you're feeling about the request**.
Stating that you're not sure you feel comfortable lets the person know that you may come back with a *no*. For example, let's say that a friend has asked you to speak to his organization about your work with handicapped children. You're passionate about what you do, but you're really not comfortable speaking to groups. When he realizes this, he may be very understanding. He may ask you to think about it and let him know by the end of the week. Or he may ask if there's someone else who would be more appropriate.

The downside of this option is that

someone who is less interested in your wellbeing may take the opportunity to pressure you. A "friend" (whom you see at social gatherings but don't spend any one-on-one time with) may immediately want to know why you're not comfortable. Don't fall for this! When someone who isn't close to you wants to know why you might not do something, it's most likely the beginning of a long "debate." Don't let someone you hardly know talk you into doing something you don't feel good about. If someone asks why, you can give a general response that reiterates your possible discomfort and your commitment to responding:

> *I'm just not sure. I need a few days to think about it.*

Repetition, as you'll see later on, is a fairly powerful way of stating your boundary. It lets the other person know that you're not backing off.

4. **You can say *I'll get back to you* – with or without a timeframe.**
Giving a timeframe lets the person know that you take the request seriously, which can make the delay more acceptable. Unless you're dealing with someone close to you, not giving a timeframe may give the impression that the request (or possibly the person) is less important to you. That shouldn't be a problem with casual requests. People who don't know you very well may see it as a

brush-off – which might not be so bad if you want to say *no*. But I don't suggest trying it on pushy or aggressive people, as they're likely to react badly. Rather give them a timeframe (sooner rather than later) and get back to them by email, text or phone.

5. **You can make a statement or ask a question. The effects are quite different.**
   When I ask whether I can check my schedule and get back to you in the morning, I'm making sure that your needs will be met. If you tell me that you need to know tonight, then I'll do my best to accommodate that. When I say, "Let's talk about it on Monday," I'm not really asking.

   When the other person has authority over you, asking is a way of acknowledging that position. When the relationship is important for other reasons, asking can be a nice way to communicate that. When the other person isn't close to you and doesn't have authority over you, asking permission is seldom a good idea. It gives others power over you – a power that they haven't earned and may abuse. You don't need the world's permission to think something over. Take all the time you need, and don't apologize for it.

Why isn't this easy for me?
You may find it difficult to take the time you need for one of these reasons:

1. **You don't want to seem unsure of yourself.** If that's the case, it's important to remember that you need time to think before

you can be sure of just about anything. Besides ... deciding too quickly can make you look like a pushover, so you might as well give yourself the time you need. You'll make a better decision that way.

2. **You're worried about offending someone.** Anyone who is offended because you need time to think doesn't have your best interests at heart. Don't give your power to that kind of person.

3. **You won't know what to say if someone demands to know why you need time.** Remember that you don't have to explain yourself to anyone (except your boss).

4. **You're used to giving people what they want.** If this is the case, then pressing the pause button is a great first step toward taking control of your life. If anyone asks why you suddenly need time, you can say that you've been making decisions too quickly.

Getting Started

The first step is often the hardest, so here are some easy ways to get started.

1. Notice who you're uncomfortable saying *no* to and ask yourself why. It's important to understand yourself first.

2. Decide ahead of time who deserves an explanation and who doesn't.

3. Practice what I call "empty explanations":
   - *I just don't want to decide right now,* or
   - *I need some time to think,* or even
   - *I'll get back to you tonight.*

These are all good ways to answer people who demand to know why you won't just give them what they want, right this minute.

4. Think about how to get back to someone. With pushy people, the more distance the better. Ask for an email or text to remind you; then it's easy to reply in the same way. If conversation is necessary, try to do it by phone. That way you don't have to deal with judgmental looks, and it should be easier to end the conversation when you've had enough.

5. Start with someone who won't argue with you. Then, once you've had some practice, you can move on to people who might try to change your mind.

Of course, buying time isn't always the answer. Sometimes all it takes is a little creativity. And that's what our next tip is all about....

Chapter 2

THE 2ᴺᴰ EASY WAY: THINK OUTSIDE THE BOX

Sometimes we don't need more time to make a good decision. We already know that the answer is *no*, even though we value the relationship. Maybe you just don't want to look at wedding dresses with your sister ... again. Maybe you don't have the time to help your cousin redesign her kitchen, even though you like doing that kind of thing. Or maybe you've done enough for this friend and he needs to manage on his own. Doing too much (or doing things we really dislike) for friends and family can leave us feeling tired and resentful – not exactly the best foundation for our relationships.

When you care about the person but aren't willing to do what they've asked of you, it's easy to think that there are only two choices: put the relationship first and ignore your own needs, or put your own needs first and ignore the relationship. This belief can leave us with an intense inner conflict – and all the difficult emotions (especially guilt and resentment) that go with it. Fortunately, there are other options.

Focus on What You Both Want

Rather than thinking about what you don't want, shift your thinking to what you **do** want. You want to help the person you care about. And you want something for yourself (free time, avoiding something unpleasant, etc.). So ask the person you care about some questions:

> *What can I do for you when you're shopping for dresses? Is it company you want? Or another opinion? Or someone to negotiate with the store owner? What would you like my help with?*

> "Well, there's this one dress at Rosalind's. I love it, but I'm worried that it makes me look fat. Would you come with me? I trust you to tell me the truth, and you never hurt my feelings."

Now that you know what she's looking for, you know you don't need to spend the entire day looking at dresses. You can give her what she wants and still avoid what you don't want. But just in case, put a boundary in place:

> *I'd be happy to go to Rosalind's with you as long as were finished by 11:00. I have to be somewhere else at 11:30.*

Your sister will be happy with this, because you'll have enough time to see her in the dress and tell her the truth (in your usual tactful way). And if she wants you to stay longer, just remind her that you need to leave by 11:00 for your next commitment. (This may be a commitment to someone else or to yourself. If you've promised yourself a quiet lunch at your favorite place, then keep your promise!)

That kitchen redesign could take all weekend, and you just don't have that kind of time. But what could you do that would help? If you don't have ideas of your own, then simply ask:

Amy, I don't have the time to do the whole kitchen with you; I've already had to keep my sister's wedding dress time to one hour. But I'd really like to help you. What do you need from me the most? What can I do for you in a fairly short time?

"Well, I've chosen what I want, but I need some help figuring out whether it will all work. I *really* need your help with that. I don't know who else to ask."

If you bring the catalogue home with all the information – including the measurements – I'd be happy to spend an hour or two with you late Saturday afternoon. I could come by around 4:00 and stay until 6:00 or so. Have an extra copy of those kitchen plans ready for us to mark up.

Your commitment is to spend up to two hours helping her to see whether the things she's chosen will fit. You do this well, so two hours is enough. And your cousin should now understand that you can't help with other aspects of it – at least not right now. If she tries to convince you to stay longer or return tomorrow, here's the kind of response that works for me:

I told you I could spend a couple of hours; that's all I have available this weekend. I'm sure things will go much better now that you understand your choices. But take your time; don't let anyone rush you into a decision. Smile, gather your things, and walk to the door.

She's probably feeling insecure about the decisions ahead of her. And you don't want to spend tomorrow accompanying her to five different showrooms while she struggles to make up her mind. You know her too well. You've set your boundary and also reminded her that there's no rush. She doesn't need to decide this weekend; the old kitchen will still be there on Monday morning.

Understand What's Really Happening

And what about that friend – the one who seems to need your assistance regularly? Joe has been asking you for a lot of help lately, and you're not sure why. He's usually more confident. He's a good friend, so why not find out what's going on?

Joe, is everything OK? You're usually so sure of yourself, but lately you seem … I don't know … almost insecure compared to the Joe I know. What's going on? (Notice the careful choice of words: "almost" insecure and only when "compared to the Joe I know.")

It turns out that Joe has been taken out of his comfort zone. He has new responsibilities at work, in a field that's new to him (but old hat to you). That's why he's been calling you so often with these questions – questions that he doesn't really know how to ask, let alone answer. He's afraid to fail, and he's afraid to admit that he feels incompetent.

You offer to spend some time in the next few days taking him through the basics so that he'll feel more comfortable. Then he'll know what he needs to ask, and he should be able to get the answers he needs without you. You'll have fewer interruptions to your workday, and Joe will regain his confidence. Everyone wins.

Look for Other Options

Your brother wants you to babysit on Friday night. You have a good relationship with him, and you enjoy spending time with his children. He doesn't ask you for much, so you'd like to help. But you work long hours during the week, and by Friday you're tired. Friday night is **your** night. You don't want to give it to anyone – especially if it means tiring yourself out even more!

You want a quiet Friday evening, but you also want to help your brother. So start with the basics:

What's happening on Friday night?

Your brother wants to surprise his wife and take her to a concert. He chose Friday because it would be nice for them to relax at the end of the week. Now that you understand his needs, it's time to express yours.

I'd love to help; you and Susan certainly deserve a night to yourselves, and I enjoy spending time with the kids. But Fridays are difficult for me. I feel drained at the end of the week, and I really need the time to relax and recharge. I'd feel overwhelmed by the kids instead of enjoying the time with them. What about Saturday night? Would that work for you?

Saturday is probably fine. And if it isn't, keep looking for more options. Maybe Mom can join you, so that you won't feel so overwhelmed (not ideal, but maybe you're willing to do it for your brother). Or maybe your brother can take his children to other relatives or friends who would be happy to look after them. You don't have to be physically present for the solution. Just help your brother to get what matters to him while still respecting your own needs.

> You don't have to be
> physically present for the solution.

Thinking out of the box is an important skill – one that we often forget to use. Just because someone wants something from you doesn't mean that's the only option. The trick is to find a solution that honors everyone – including you. Often this is easier than it seems. And when it isn't … well, there are still five more tips to help you keep those important boundaries in place!

Why isn't this easy for me?
You may struggle with this for a number of reasons:
1. **You've been brought up to think of things in black and white.** If you've grown up with all-or-nothing thinking, you may be used to

saying either *yes* or *no*. Make a habit of asking yourself what other options there are.

2. **You're used to putting others first.** Remember that you're not ignoring the needs of others; you're figuring out how to help them while still respecting yourself. If you don't respect your own needs, you'll end up angry and resentful. And trust me – no one will enjoy that!

3. **People need you.** This may (or may not) be true. But what do they really need you for? This process allows you to go where you're most needed and leave the rest to someone else.

4. **You owe someone.** Most of us owe someone at some point in our lives. But that doesn't mean you have to do their bidding. Of course you want to repay the favor ... but it's up to you how to do that.

Getting Started

1. **Ask a good friend to help you.** Practice discussing options together. Maybe your friend can help you learn to think more creatively.

2. **Get more comfortable talking about what you want.** If you and a friend always go to the same restaurant, let her know that you'd like to try something else. If you're used to just going along with the crowd, start expressing your opinion more often. Then, when your brother wants you to babysit on a Friday, you'll find it easier to tell him why Friday doesn't work for you.

3. **Ask for ideas.** People who care about you understand that you can't always be there to help. The next time one of them asks for something inconvenient, be honest. Share your thoughts and ask what else you could do to help.

Thinking outside the box is an important skill, especially when you're dealing with family, friends, or a boss with unrealistic expectations. After all, there are only so many hours in the day. But what can you do when you suspect that you should just say *no* – but you're not quite sure or don't know how? Don't worry; that's what the rest of this book is for. Our next tip will help you to figure out when you're being manipulated by charm or flattery – and what to do about it.

Chapter 3

THE 3RD EASY WAY: DON'T FALL FOR CHARM AND FLATTERY

Charm and flattery work by making us feel good; manipulators use both. They're effective because they trigger powerful emotions that hijack our brains. We don't think clearly until those emotions subside, making us all too easy to control.

It's important to understand the difference between compliments and flattery. "I like your new haircut," and "That was a great presentation," are compliments. To qualify as flattery, compliments must be excessive or insincere. If we don't see through it (and sometimes even if we do), flattery can make us feel good for a little while. Manipulators know the value of those good feelings, so they keep them coming – as long as we do what they want.

While flattery is all about the words, charm can be considered a way of being. Charming people make you feel comfortable, perhaps even special, in their presence. While flattery is artificial, charm may be perfectly genuine. And because it's more subtle than flattery, it can be hard to tell the difference.

How Flattery Works

Flattery is designed to make us feel good about ourselves and to try to hold onto that feeling as long as possible. It works best on people who are looking for approval or tend to doubt themselves.

> Flattery works best on people
> who are looking for approval.

Although any topic is fair game, manipulators who use flattery often tell us how unique we are and how much they depend on us. For example:

"You're the only one who can make this happen."

"You always create the perfect atmosphere. Little Susie's party just wouldn't be the same without your creative touch."

"I know I can count on you when I'm in a pinch. I don't know what I'd do without you."

"You're the only one I trust with this."

These comments are designed to make us feel special and appreciated, which can be quite effective if we don't feel that way very often. Because those nice feelings are connected with the manipulator, we find it hard to say *no*.

Have Some Responses Ready (Four Examples to Give You Ideas)

Here are some simple but effective ways to respond to inappropriate flattery:

"You're the only one who can make this happen."

Actually, I'm not. John is a much better choice. He has both the contacts and the skills to pull this off. I have the skills, but not the contacts. And cold-calling just isn't for me.

In this example, you've explained why someone else is a better choice – and why you're not willing to get involved.

"You always create the perfect atmosphere. Little Susie's party just wouldn't be the same without your creative touch."

Thanks for the compliment. But you're also very creative. Joanne's going-away party was absolutely beautiful. I'll be happy to send you links to the websites I use for children's events. Just looking at the pictures will give you plenty of ideas!

Here the most important piece of information ("you're also very creative") turns out to be a compliment. So you've returned the compliment and offered to share your trade secrets. If that isn't enough to close the deal, just let your friend know how confident you are in her abilities. Finish the conversation by promising to send the websites first thing in the morning. And if you're willing, you can always offer to throw around some ideas with her. Sharing ideas is a lot easier than doing the job yourself.

"I know I can count on you when I'm in a pinch. I don't know what I'd do without you."

I can't help you this time. But you'll do just fine without me.

This tactic contains a double whammy: the power of flattery *and* the power of guilt. He knows he can count on you because you've bailed him out before – far too many times, in fact.

Taking responsibility for someone else's mistakes on a regular basis is not a badge of honor. It's a pattern that leads to anger and resentment – and often prevents us from doing the things that truly matter to us.

Some people are perpetually rescuing others from their own mistakes because it makes them feel needed. If this is true for you, then it's time to work on your self-esteem. When you feel good about yourself, you need less of what psychologists call *external validation.* (This is anything from outside of ourselves that makes us feel valuable.) When you value yourself, it doesn't matter so much whether others need you or not. What matters is the quality of your relationships.

---

*Taking responsibility for someone
else's mistakes on a regular basis
is not a badge of honor.*

Some people believe that a good person helps others whenever possible, putting her own needs at the bottom of the list. This is a good belief to question. When people don't fulfill their responsibilities, is it really a good idea to rescue them? Chances are you're just helping them to remain irresponsible.

Are you regularly giving up things you enjoy, or that matter to you, in order to be a good person? If so, then it might be time to revisit your definition of *good person.* Think about the people you admire, whether you know them personally or not. Those who give the most to the world usually offer it on their own terms. They don't let others choose for them.

And once you've established what you most admire, look within and acknowledge those qualities in yourself. You probably have more of them than you've ever given yourself credit for.

"You're the only one I trust with this. No one else will get it right."

Actually, I'm not the only one who can do it — just the one who always does. It's time someone else stepped up.

This approach can be useful when you've had enough. You've managed all of the events for this group for far too long, and you find yourself resenting it. It seems that everyone assumes you'll take care of things; no one even bothers to say *please* or *thank you* any more.

You could suggest other people who would do the job well. You could even offer to help someone the first time through. But be careful. If you think you'll get roped into doing most of the work, then let whoever is responsible for filling the position deal with it. Listen to your gut. You'll know what's best.

Remember that people who feel comfortable with themselves aren't so easily flattered. If flattery works a little too well on you, you may need to put some time and energy into your self-image. Knowing your strengths and accepting your weaknesses will make it harder for people to manipulate you with false praise.

How Charm Works

Charm is a bit hard to define, but we all know it when we experience it. You know you're being charmed when you enjoy someone's company and want more of it. If there's no agenda, it's harmless. But some of these people want more than your company. They want to get you hooked on the good feelings they produce. They want you to become so dependent on those feelings that you'll do whatever it takes to keep them coming.

I call these people charmers. They tend to be good listeners and great conversationalists. They quickly learn how you think and what you care about, so you always find them interesting. They make you laugh with their funny stories or impress you with their accomplishments and adventures. And they pay attention to you, noticing the little things that others miss. They may use flattery, although the clever ones don't need it. You feel so good when they're around that you naturally want to spend more time with them. Before you know it, you're hooked.

So how do you know whether someone's charm is genuine? How do you tell the difference between a kind, caring person and a heartless manipulator? Don't worry. There are signs.

First of all, pay attention to your feelings – especially early on. If something doesn't feel right, check it out. **Don't wait.** The more time you spend with a charmer, the more likely you are to forget or ignore those early warning signs.

By definition, charming people are easy to get along with. The genuine ones respect others; they tend to be more accepting of differences than most people. They're interested in different points of view, and they don't need everyone to agree with them. They're great company because see the good in everything. And they're usually great storytellers.

Charmers are more concerned with how they come across to others. Rather than acknowledging and accepting differences, they tend to agree with others, at least superficially. You may wonder what they really believe, because you've heard them agree with so many different ideas. Like their genuine counterparts, they're interested in your point of view – but only because agreeing with it keeps them in your good graces. They're great company because they see the good in whomever they're trying to charm. (And if they don't see anything, they'll make up something.)

And what about the stories? A charmer's stories will usually make him look clever or adventurous or well-connected. A genuinely charming person will most likely have a variety of stories, including plenty that make others look good. They share their stories for the pure enjoyment of it, not because they need to impress you.

Charm is harder to spot than flattery, so don't feel like a fool if a charmer has gotten her hooks into you. It can happen to anyone. If you're unsure of yourself, contemplate these question:

- Am I doing anything for her that makes me uncomfortable?
- Am I ignoring my feelings or making excuses for her?
- Are the people close to me worried about this relationship?

Genuinely charming people are a great gift, and they don't ask too much of you. If you're worried that someone is using charm to influence you, take that concern seriously. Think about it carefully, and get input from someone you trust. If you don't ask the right questions now, you may regret it later.

Why isn't this easy for me?

Charm and flattery work better on some people than others. If you think you're one of those people, consider these possibilities:

1. **You're looking for approval.** People who lack confidence in themselves or their decisions are the best targets for this type of manipulation. Flattery can distract you from self-doubt, making you feel better for a while.

2. **You don't feel good about yourself.** When your self-esteem is low, it feels great to spend time with someone who appreciates you just the way you are. A talented charmer conveys this appreciation indirectly, by the quality of his attention. He notices the little things about you that others miss; he's interested in your thoughts and feelings. He shows you how special you are by the way he treats you.

3. **You're lonely.** Whether it's because you're new in town or you're just shy, loneliness is hard. And there's no better cure for it than some positive attention. Enjoy the company; just make sure you're comfortable with the choices you're making.

Getting Started

The first step is to recognize charmers and flatterers – not always an easy task. Here are some ideas:

1. **Pay attention to the compliments you're getting.** Flattery is defined as "excessive or insincere praise" and it can be tough to spot. Consider asking a trusted friend to help you figure it out.

2. **Remember the difference between genuine and artificial charm.** Do his stories make others look good, or only himself? Is he willing to share his own opinions, or is he a

yes-man? Does he see the good in the world, or only in the person he's talking to?

3. **Notice your feelings.** Do you want to be around someone a little too much? This can be a warning sign (although it also happens when we fall in love). Ask yourself what makes you feel so good.

4. **Notice what you're doing for others and why**. If you're worried that someone may be trying to manipulate you, look at what you're doing for him. Are you going "above and beyond"? If so, pay more attention to the nature of the relationship. Is there more give than take? Are you doing anything that you wouldn't normally do for a friend?

If someone is using flattery to manipulate you, go back to that section and try out some of the responses I've suggested. If you're falling for someone's charms (rather than his virtues), consider putting some distance between the charmer and yourself until the spell wears off. And work on your self-esteem. Once you stop doubting yourself, charmers will find it much more difficult to get what they want from you.

Of course, not all manipulation comes wrapped up in charm. Some people lie, others make you feel like a bad person, and others simply demand to know why you won't do their bidding. ("What could possibly be more important than this?") In our next tip, we'll look at what happens when you explain too much – and how to prevent those endless "debates" that you can never win.

Chapter 4

THE 4TH EASY WAY: NO EXCUSES, NO JUSTIFICATIONS

You have the right to remain silent.
Anything you say can and will be used against you.

Some people will use anything you say against you. When you give them an excuse for not helping out, they'll come up with a way to rearrange your life so that you can still accommodate them. Or they'll become indignant at the mere thought that something else (even your family or your integrity) could be more important than their needs. Then they'll let you know, directly or indirectly, what a bad person you are to even consider refusing them.

Or perhaps they'll keep reminding you of all the reasons that their needs are so important – implying that whatever they want is more important than your other priorities. But because they're not saying anything directly, they don't have to tell you which of those priorities you should sacrifice for them. This strategy usually works well with people who believe they must put others first; they simply give up what little time they have for themselves and do what everyone else wants.

Don't hand over your power!

Don't say too much. Making excuses means handing your power to others; it suggests you must justify yourself to them. Unless you're dealing with someone in authority, say as little as possible. Don't let anyone talk you into something you'll regret later.

Here are some ways to hold on to your power and just say *no*:

> *I can't help you with that.*
> *I won't be there.*
> *You'll have to manage without me this time.*
> *I'm not taking on any more commitments for a couple of weeks. If you still need help after the 15th, talk to me then and I'll see what I can do.*
> *I'd really like to help you get that job. But I can't recommend someone who doesn't have the experience they require.*

If the attempts continue, simply repeat your decision, either in the same words or with something similar:

> *I [still] can't help you.*
> *I won't be there.*
> *I understand. And you'll have to manage without me. If you still need help after the 15th, I'll see what I can do.*
> *I wish I could help, but you don't have the right experience.*

What if they keep insisting?

"That's all fine," you're thinking, "but what do I do when the arguments start? How do I manage to avoid excuses and justifications when someone demands them ... or just gives me that look?"

It's actually easier than it sounds. Take a nice, deep breath and remind yourself of this simple truth: "Just because someone demands an explanation doesn't mean you have to provide one."

Just because someone demands
an explanation doesn't mean
you have to provide one.

Yes, I'm completely serious. Everyone wants what they want. But no one has the right to decide what's private for you and what isn't. Only **you** can decide how much information you share ... and with whom.

Sharing information whenever someone demands it puts that person in charge of the conversation (as well as whatever's left of your privacy). Before you know it, you're giving them whatever they want just to make that conversation end. Don't let someone else control the conversation; they'll end up controlling you.

When someone demands an explanation, there are many ways to let them know that you're not going to provide one. Here are some options:

I can't help you with that.

"Why not?"

I just can't.

"But why?"

I've already told you – I just can't.

I won't be there.

"But it won't be the same without you! Why can't you make it?"

I just can't.

"Why won't you talk to me about it?"

I just don't want to talk about it. But thanks for thinking of me. (This is a good time to change the subject or say a friendly goodbye.)

You'll have to manage without me this time.

"But I need you! You can make time for me!"

Not right now.

"What's so important that you can't help me?"

I have other things to take care of.

"Other things? What's more important than this?"

The other things I'm busy taking care of.

Using the same words ("other things" and "take care of") adds power to your message. If the pressure continues, consider a more direct statement: *I'm not going into the details.*

I'm not taking on any more commitments for a couple of weeks. If you still need help after the 15th, talk to me then and I'll see what I can do.

"But I can't wait until the 15th. I need your help now!"

I understand, and I wish I could help you. But I'm not taking on anything else until after the 15th.

42

You don't have the right experience.
"But they could make an exception. That's why I need your help!"
I'm sorry to disappoint you, but the answer is no.
If the pleading continues, you can make a stronger statement: *Please don't ask again; my decision is final.* Or just walk away.

As these examples illustrate, you can choose to tell someone directly that you won't be sharing your reasons, or you can simply restate your original response. Either way, you're letting them know that it's **your** decision. And it's not negotiable.

But what about "the look"?

Instead of arguing, the other person may just look at you as if to say, "You don't really mean that, do you? No decent person would refuse me!" What do you do then?

The answer is simple. Become comfortable with silence … and other people's judgments, opinions and attitudes. Their opinions belong to them, not you.

If you're not comfortable with silence, and you're taking on the judgments that you imagine are behind that look, then you will naturally start making excuses in order to fill the gap – and make those awful feelings go away. Don't do it!

"The look" (and the silence that goes with it) is only a useful weapon as long as you're intimidated by it. My experience with clients and workshop participants tells me that it's not the silence we're uncomfortable with – it's the difficult feelings about ourselves that the silence brings up. What comes up

43

for you during that silence? Do you feel guilty? Do you want that person to approve of you, to tell you it's OK? Or do you feel frightened? Perhaps saying *no* wasn't safe when you were growing up. Did an angry parent physically or verbally abuse you when you said it?

It's not the silence we're
uncomfortable with – it's the
difficult feelings about ourselves.

Many people can become more comfortable with silence with some practice and perseverance. If you find that you can't, or that the feelings it brings up are just too uncomfortable, then get some help with your emotions. It's time to take back control of your life.

When someone gives you "the look," you can choose to respond in a number of different ways. You can look straight back, firmly and comfortably – sending a clear message that you're not intimidated. Stay with the silence for a bit, just to reinforce that "I'm not intimidated" message. Then change the subject or say goodbye.

Another option is to restate your decision, or wish the person the best of luck, and walk away. (Walking away is usually the best option when you're dealing with toxic people.) This can be a good choice if you're not comfortable with silence yet. I also like its simplicity and efficiency. Walking away puts an end to the unpleasantness and reinforces your decision.

You can also call people on their behavior, which not only lets them know that "the look" isn't working, but that it won't work next time, either. But I'm getting ahead of myself. That's our next tip....

Stand your ground!

With a bit of practice, you'll need excuses less and less. Excuses are another way of giving away your power. When the relationship doesn't justify it, making excuses tells the other person that you want him to be satisfied with your decision. You need his approval – which he can (and often will) withhold.

Looking for agreement or approval opens the door to endless debate ... the kind you'll do just about anything to avoid. Learn to stand your ground without over-explaining yourself, and you'll transform some of your most difficult relationships.

Why isn't this easy for me?

Many of us are in the habit of justifying ourselves, and it can be quite difficult to stop. Here are some of the reasons:

1. **You feel rude not explaining yourself.** Keep reminding yourself that you don't owe the world an explanation. Save your reasons for the people who care enough about you to respect your decisions.

2. **You're not used to taking control of the conversation.** Think about the price you pay for letting a manipulator take charge.

3. **You want people to understand and agree with your decision.** Remember that some people will never approve until you do exactly what they want. These people don't care what

you think, so why should you worry about what they think?

Getting Started

1. **Be clear about what's private for you and what isn't.** For some people, money is private. For others, it's their romantic relationships. And for others, it's just about everything. Knowing yourself is the first step.

2. **Identify the people who demand explanations that they're not entitled to.** Just naming these people will help you to become more aware – and less likely to give them information that's none of their business.

3. **Practice different ways of refusing to explain yourself.** There are lots of examples in this chapter. Go through them and see what works for you. Change the words as much as you like and practice saying them until you feel more comfortable.

4. **Take a few deep breaths before explaining yourself.** This will give you time to think about whether that's really such a good idea.

Demanding an explanation is only one tactic in the manipulator's bag of tricks. In the next two tips, we'll explore a whole bunch of manipulation strategies and the best ways to deal with them. As we'll see, there is no single best way. It all depends on what you want ... and how likely you are to get it.

Chapter 5

THE 5TH ~~EASY~~ WAY: HANDLE MANIPULATION DIRECTLY

Many of us have people in our lives who manipulate us regularly. These people are masters at distorting the truth – or getting us to distort it for them through our insecurities and self-doubt. If there's someone like this in your life, and you're not willing or able to stay out of contact, then you may need to take the bull by the horns.

A Friendly Warning: You may find some of these approaches difficult. If you're uncomfortable with these suggestions, consider the more subtle approaches in the next chapter. They're much gentler and easier.

If you're dealing with a truly toxic person – the kind who consistently refuses to take responsibility for her actions and tries to make you feel guilty for even suggesting the possibility – the direct approach will only make things worse. Toxic people don't admit their mistakes, and they don't change their ways. This method is for difficult people, not totally unreasonable ones.

I also suggest using this approach only when needed, as things may become quite unpleasant. Use it when you feel you can handle the disapproval and guilt-tripping that's likely to follow – or that it's worth it anyway.

Manipulation is a topic worthy of an entire book, but this tip and the next make a great introduction. Let's start with the example from the previous tip: "the look."

So far we've seen how to stop this tactic in the moment. But what if you want to put an end to it for good? What if you're sick and tired of "the look" and want to make it perfectly clear that you're not giving in to it any longer? This can be a good time for the direct approach.

I'm not sure how to interpret the look on your face. Are you trying to tell me something?

"You're imagining things. There's no particular 'look' on my face."

Good. I just needed to be sure. Now change the subject. Do **not** debate whether you were imagining things. It's unpleasant, and it gives the other person far too much power. You know your truth; why debate it with someone who's trying to intimidate you? This simple response lets people know that you're aware of their tricks ... and that you're not afraid to deal with them head on. The "look" will not work with you.

Of course, the conversation may not go so easily. The response from the other person may be more aggressive:

"*Look*?! What *look*? Honestly, you're always imagining I'm up to something!"

I just needed to be sure. Saying this in a calm, even voice makes it clear that the speaker's accusations and emotional tone cannot be used to control you. Now change the subject or walk away. As I've already mentioned, do not begin (or get sucked into) an argument here; it's one you can never win. Fortunately you don't need to.

What are you trying to prove?

Making accusations is just another manipulation tactic. Getting hooked into it emotionally gives the other person the power they're looking for. To stay in control of the conversation, you need to let go of the need to prove yourself to anyone. Yes, you read that right: **Let go of the need to prove yourself to anyone.** Until you do, others have far too much power over you.

I did warn you, didn't I? Parts of this approach may not seem so easy! But letting go of the need to prove yourself is worth the effort. It will change your life.

Letting go of the need to
prove yourself will change your life.

Manipulation takes many forms; "the look" is just one of them. Here are some of the more common ones, along with some ways to deal with them directly. Remember, the reason to address manipulation directly is to stop people from using these tactics on you again. You're pushing them out of their comfort zone, so don't expect them to love you for it.

Stop that guilt trip in its tracks!

If you're susceptible to guilt, the people who know this have power over you. They've learned through experience that you'll give them what they want in order to make that horrible feeling go away. Here are some examples, along with some ways to stop them in their tracks:

"You're the only one who will help me. No one else cares."

This is a classic "poor me" scenario, with you as the hero. If you feel sorry for the underdog, then this one will pull on your heartstrings. Watch out or you'll feel terribly sorry for this poor victim ... and painfully guilty until you agree to do whatever he's asking.

If this is not his first "poor me," then chances are it won't be his last. If you feel it's time to put an end to this tactic, here are some options for you:

That's not true. Plenty of people care. They're just not willing to keep doing things that you're responsible for. And neither am I. This is quite direct – maybe a bit too direct for comfort. Remember its purpose. You're not trying to make someone feel good; you're putting an end to this particular type of manipulation. Warm, fuzzy words will not accomplish your goal.

If you feel uncomfortable but feel you need to say

it anyway, you can walk away once the words are out of your mouth.

Here's another way to deal with this tactic:

People caring or not caring about you is not the issue. You can't expect people to drop what they're doing at the last minute because you didn't plan properly. That goes for me as well. Again, this is not a "feel good" response, and you may want to walk away once you've delivered it. If you want this person to feel good right now, then continue to do his bidding. He'll be very happy!

In both of these examples, you've made it clear that the "poor me" routine will not succeed with you. You've set a foundation for future interactions.

I'd like to end with one of my personal favorites:

"How can you be so selfish?"

What this really means is, "How can you put your needs before mine?" Take a deep breath and remind yourself of this. With this new understanding, all sorts of great responses come to mind. Here are just a few:

I'm not going to feel guilty for putting my needs ahead of yours once in a while. Here you're using the "g" word. You've named the tactic and directly stated that you won't be giving in to it. You've also suggested that you've put the other person first more often than you should. It doesn't get much clearer than this.

Here's a gentler way to say the same thing:

I know you're not used to me thinking of myself. But it's time I did. Here you refuse to accept the label of "selfish" and let the manipulator know that you've changed your way of thinking. From now on, you'll be considering your own needs as well. Expect to encounter further resistance, but stick with it. You'll feel so much better about yourself!

And here's an all-purpose response to guilt trips:

I've been doing things out of guilt for years. My dues are more than paid. There's that "g" word again! You've made it clear that your guilt has passed its sell-by date. Using it to manipulate you just won't work.

There are, of course, many other ways that people try to make us feel guilty. Let's look at a very popular one: our sense of obligation.

Obligation: Check in with Your Gut

Are you doing things for people purely because you feel obligated? If so, keep this in mind: **Obligations don't last forever. At some point you've done enough. It's up to you to decide when you've reached that point. And if you haven't, it's up to you to decide how to get there.**

Doing something for you does not give me the right to decide what you must do for me (or when you must do it). The best criteria are your own feelings about what's right, or your desire to help –

not my feelings of entitlement. Obligation does not equal ownership.

Obligation does not equal ownership.

Obligation does not equal ownership.

Sometimes we do things out of obligation even though the other person doesn't expect us to. At other times people remind us, directly or indirectly, that we owe them ... and they expect their payback **now**. When this is happening, and we feel that it's unfair, we may need to address it directly. Here are some examples to help you find the words to express what's true for you:

You're right, I do owe you. You really came through for me when I needed it. But lying goes against my values. I don't owe you that. I've never asked you to compromise your integrity for me. Don't ask me to do so for you.

I do owe you. But I have a deadline at the office and I can't afford to miss it. Please don't ask me to put my career on the line in order to repay a favor. I can't do it.

In both of these examples, you've clearly stated the limits of your obligation. You've given your reasons for refusing without apologies or excuses. And you've done so in a way that makes a reasonable argument nearly impossible.

What do you do when you consider the debt paid? How do you handle those people who insist that you still owe them ... when you've been repaying the same debt for years?

This is a difficult situation, and if you want to be free of it you'll need to face it. As long as you refuse to challenge the assumption that you owe more than you could ever repay, the demands will continue. If you're ready to put a stop to it, then you'll need to clearly state your boundaries.

Let's say that some relatives helped you when you were in your teens and your mother was ill for two years. But that was twenty years ago, and they've been taking advantage of your time and resources ever since. Now they want you to get them tickets to a sold-out performance – tickets that you can get, but that are reserved for important clients. You already have more clients than pairs of tickets. What do you say?

I simply can't. Those tickets are reserved for clients, and I'm already going to disappoint some of them. There just aren't enough to go around.

Here comes the guilt trip: "After all we've done for you? Certainly you can find a way. It would mean so much to us …."

You know how much I appreciate all of the support you gave me when my mother was ill. I've always done what I can to show my gratitude – even twenty years later. But I can't spend my whole life paying off that debt. I need those tickets for my biggest clients, and I just don't have any to spare.

Here you're acknowledging their role in your life and your gratitude to them. You then set your boundary: that you can't owe them forever (it was, after all, twenty years ago) and you won't allow them to interfere with your relationship with your clients.

Expect that the next time they want something they'll remind you of how disappointed they were – and expect you to compensate for it. Don't feel guilty for finally bringing some balance into the relationship. Stand your ground, and don't agree to do things that you don't want to do – including spending time with them if you don't enjoy it.

What will you do for approval?
Some of us want approval so much that we'll do just about anything to get it. Realize that the approval you get from doing others' bidding is temporary. It only lasts until your services are needed again, because your relationship is all about them. Consider walking away from these one-sided relationships.

Sometimes people we're close to use this tactic, and ending the relationship isn't an option we're willing to consider. What then?

> **"I thought you were a good daughter. I didn't think that a little social event would stand in the way of that."**
>
> *My high school reunion is important to me. It's not OK to suggest that I'm not a good daughter because I'm not willing to miss it. Let's see who else can take you to the dinner.*

If you want to be more polite (in other words, less direct), you can skip the second sentence entirely. I've included it here because this chapter is about dealing with manipulation directly. That sentence lets your mother know, in no uncertain terms, that you see what's she up to and you won't put up with it. But it won't stop overnight. You'll have to keep calling her on it until she gets the message.

Notice that my response didn't address the difference between a high school reunion and a "little social event." There's no need to point out all the ways that someone's statements are bad or wrong. Focus on what's most important and stick with that.

"I thought you were a good…" makes it clear what's at stake. Give her what she wants, or you won't get her approval. A great teacher once taught me that what other people think of you is none of your business. Don't let anyone, even family, use their judgments, opinions or feelings about your choices against you. And don't measure yourself by them, either.

Of course, approval isn't always about words. When someone uses a disapproving tone to control you, you may be tempted to call him on it. But he'll probably just deny it – and that's an argument you'll never win. In this case, an "almost direct" approach might be more effective:

> *That tone of voice reminds me of when my father used to scold us as kids* [replace this with whatever memory is appropriate]. *I just need a moment to think clearly.* Pause briefly (or longer, if you're feeling strong emotions or need more time to think). I suggest using a matter-of-fact tone, completely free of apologies. You're simply explaining how this tone affects you and taking a moment (or two or three) to recover.

Of course, there's still room for denial: "Tone? What tone? There's nothing wrong with my 'tone'!" Simply point out that you weren't complaining. That tone of voice just takes you back to unpleasant childhood memories, and you need a moment. Do this every time someone uses his tone of voice as a weapon, and eventually he'll learn that it simply doesn't work.

Other people expect you to live up to their standards. To live a fulfilling life, you must set your own standards. You're the only one who must be comfortable with your choices. Live according to your own highest values and you will be.

Don't give in to intimidation!

Intimidation takes many forms: body language, tone of voice, yelling, and all kinds of threats. If someone threatens you physically, do not put yourself at risk. Get away as soon as possible – and stay away.

When you're not in physical danger, here are some options to consider:

> *It feels like you're trying to intimidate me. I don't give in to intimidation.* This may trigger all kinds of unpleasant responses, as no one enjoys being accused of intimidation. In most cases, you can reiterate that this is how it feels to you, and it's not OK.

You have the right to be treated with respect. It's up to you to insist on it.

If someone starts yelling or screaming at you, feel free to end the conversation immediately and resume it when the person is able to speak calmly. Some people use the voice as a weapon, while others shout because they've lost control. They're not necessarily trying to manipulate you; they're just feeling incredibly angry (perhaps to the point of rage) and overwhelmed. Either way, feel free to end the conversation so that you aren't subjected to verbal abuse. You have the right to be treated with respect. It's up to you to insist on it.

> *I know you're upset, but I'm not willing to let you yell at me. We can talk later, when you're less upset, or you can send me an email or text. You can get back to me whenever you're ready.*

Of course, there are many more manipulation strategies and many, many ways to deal with them. What are you faced with? If one of your challenges hasn't been covered here, it might be helpful to write down the tactic you're dealing with and your possible options. Consider what you want from the situation, as well as some of the principles discussed here, when evaluating your options. You could even write down the pros and cons of each; often that can help you to think of something even better. And if the same negative keeps coming up ("He just won't listen!"), consider what to do when that happens.

The most important thing is that you recognize manipulation for what it is and refuse to be controlled by it. Stand up for yourself in whatever way is best for you.

Why isn't this easy for me?

Calling people out won't make you popular, but sometimes it's necessary. Of course, only you can decide when the benefits outweighs the costs. Here are some of the challenges you may face:

1. **You're afraid of conflict or rejection.** No matter how respectfully you go about it, you're still telling someone that what he's doing isn't OK. If he's not mature enough to handle that, he may resort to yelling, screaming or insults in order to force you to back down.

2. **You were raised to be polite.** For many of us, being polite means avoiding unpleasant topics and pretending that everything's OK when it isn't. But good manners should be about respect, not avoidance. Respecting others means that, when there's a problem, you focus on the action rather than the person. Calling someone a liar is disrespectful. But pointing out a lie – or the consequences of future lies – is not. Keeping things pleasant isn't about good manners; it's about avoiding discomfort. If comfort is your top priority, you'll be an easy mark for manipulators.

3. **You're dealing with an unreasonable person.** In this case, the direct approach will only make things worse. There are only a few effective approaches to unreasonable people: (1) avoid dealing with them in the first place; (2) avoid things that you know will set them off, and (3) walk away from their ugliness.

Getting Started

1. **Look at your relationships.** Is there someone in your life who just can't take a hint? If you want results, you'll probably need to be direct with this person.

2. **Look at yourself.** Do you doubt yourself? Are people distracting you with guilt and personal attacks? Becoming more aware of this will make it easier to stop defending yourself and stick to the real issue.

3. **Keep your focus on what matters the most and let go of the details**. Don't overwhelm someone with a list of complaints; you're just begging for a defensive reaction. Stay focused on what really matters and save the rest for another day – or accept it as part of life.

4. **Figure out what you're so afraid of.** If you can't bring yourself to be direct, you must be afraid of something. Name it, then name the price you pay for keeping quiet. If the price is too high, you'll need to deal with that fear.

5. **Look at the situation carefully.** Analyze what's happening. Seeing the disrespect clearly may give you the courage to stand up for yourself.

If you don't feel ready for any of this, don't force yourself. Go on to the next chapter, which is filled with more polite things to say. Return here when and if the gentle approach doesn't get the results you want.

Chapter 6

THE 6TH EASY WAY: HANDLE MANIPULATION POLITELY

In the last tip, I shared ways to address manipulation quite directly. This often involved naming the tactic that was being used ("I won't feel guilty …"), making it clear that you understand the person's strategy and will not allow it to succeed.

Sometimes you don't want to be that direct. You may be worried about the consequences. You may have a strong need to be polite. (Some of us just can't be that direct, even when the other person's behavior is beyond inappropriate.) You may not want to deal with the inevitable denial and aggression. Or you may believe you can get the results you want without all that unpleasantness.

A Gentler Approach

So for those people and those times, here are some responses you may feel more comfortable with. They're designed to minimize the likelihood of confrontation, so you won't be directly suggesting that anyone said or did anything inappropriate. But don't worry ... they'll still make your point.

Let's look at some of the examples from the last tip, making them a bit kinder and gentler this time. We'll start with that personal favorite of mine:

"How can you be so selfish?"

Remember what this really means: "How can you put your needs before mine?" Once you've taken that deep breath and reminded yourself of this, here are some polite ways to let people know that this strategy just won't work with you:

> *Sometimes I need to put my own needs first. This is one of those times.* You've made it clear that you won't accept the other's arbitrary labels. You haven't come out and accused the speaker of a guilt trip, but it's obvious that you're not falling for it.

> *How interesting ... I'm actually starting to feel guilty about putting my own needs first. I guess I'm just not used to it yet. Let me know if you need anything after the 15th, and I'll see what I can do.* Then leave, hang up or (if neither of these is an option) change the subject. You've made your point: this attempt to make me feel guilty isn't working, even though I do feel uncomfortable. I'm maintaining my boundary in spite of the discomfort.

What makes these responses less direct – and more polite? In both cases, you've put everything in terms of yourself. There are no accusations, no statements about the inappropriateness of the other person's words, actions, or feelings. The focus is on you, so wounded egos and aggressive responses are less likely.

Let's look at some other polite responses. Their purpose is to be less confrontational while still setting a strong boundary regarding manipulation.

"You're the only one who will help me. No one else cares."

Actually, you can manage without me. And if there's a problem, you'll learn from the experience. One way or another, I know you'll get there.

You've reframed this into a learning experience; success may require a bit more time and effort than anticipated. You've made it clear that you're not going to drop your other priorities in order to make things easier. And you've expressed confidence in the other person's capabilities. "I know you'll get there" sums this up nicely.

If you get any argument, just keep saying, "I know you'll get there," or "You'll figure it out," until one of you tires out and ends the conversation.

Notice that this response ignores the "poor me" statement that no one else cares. The speaker will probably continue using this tactic with you. Keep ignoring it. It may just go away.

And what about the "be my hero and help me again" strategy? It probably won't disappear overnight, but you have made it quite clear that you don't sympathize with the speaker's desire to be rescued from the hard work of life.

I can feel the temptation to say 'yes' just to make you happy. But it wouldn't be right for me to make a promise that I can't keep. This lets the other person know that guilt won't work. If you said *yes* just to shut her up, you wouldn't keep your word. But it's oh-so-polite, because it puts everything in terms of her needs.

Handling Criticism and Disapproval

Let's look at some responses to other situations. In the last chapter, I suggested this response to a critical or disapproving tone of voice:

That tone of voice reminds me of when my father used to scold us as kids [replace this with whatever memory is appropriate]. *I just need a moment to think clearly.* Pause briefly (or longer, if you're feeling strong emotions or just need more time to think). I suggest using a matter-of-fact tone, completely free of apologies. You're simply stating how this tone affects you and taking a moment to recover.

If this is too direct for you, consider taking a deep breath and saying that you need a moment to think. You can do the same thing for a disapproving look, or for anything else that you find difficult. No explanation needed.

When you're ready, restate whatever the person said in a neutral way and respond to that:

I believe you were saying that Joe needs our help. I don't agree. I think he needs to take responsibility for his mistakes. But if he wants to talk about his options, I'd be happy to make myself available.

When you want to show someone that the critical tone isn't working, this is about as polite as you can get. There's no blame, and you're not threatening anyone.

When You'd Like to Help

Sometimes you'd like to help, but for some reason you just can't. Not everyone understands your needs, so here's a polite response to someone who expects you to help tomorrow morning – all morning – regardless of your schedule:

> *I really want to help; you've done so much for us. But I have commitments tomorrow that I can't break. Give me a bit more notice next time ... two or three days should be enough ... and I'll do whatever I can.* This works when you would help out if you could. You're not saying *no* to the relationship – just the last-minute nature of the request.

This response is softer than most; that's because it's intended for people whom you would choose to help under better circumstances. You're letting the other person know that he's important to you. And you're being very clear about what you're saying *no* to: not having enough time to plan. If you get any resistance after this, simply repeat that you have commitments you can't break. And if anyone demands to know what's so important, remember that your commitments are no one's business – unless you want them to be. You decide how much information to share and with whom.

Understanding Manipulation – and Yourself

If manipulation is a big part of your life, you may want to understand it better. A great way to do this is to watch TV series with manipulative characters. Analyze their tactics as well as the other characters' responses. Figure out what's happening when the manipulation succeeds – and when it doesn't.

To better understand yourself, notice the characters you relate to. Take special note of your feelings toward the "victims" who are always being manipulated. Do you feel sorry for them? What goes through your mind when you watch other characters taking advantage of them? What do you believe about them? What do you believe about those other characters?

Of course, you could do this exercise with yourself and the people in your own life. But sometimes it's easier to start in the world of make-believe. Either way, what you learn about yourself will be more than worth the effort.

Why isn't this easy for me?

Even though everything in this chapter is polite, you may still find it difficult for a number of reasons:

1. **Standing up for yourself can be hard, even with the best words.** If you can't seem to bring yourself to do it, even when the words are there, you might want to get some help dealing with your emotions. They've probably been running your life for a while.

2. **It's hard to be polite when you're feeling angry.** Sometimes you've just had enough – of a person, of a situation, of being taken for

granted. Whether you feel your anger is justified or not, it still gets in the way. If you find it hard to be polite, but you know that you need to be, buy yourself some time (see the first tip for lots of easy ways to do that). Then deal with the anger. Sometimes the person we're really angry with is right there in the mirror. After all, no one can manipulate you without your consent.

3. **Even when you're polite, there's still the risk of a confrontation.** Unreasonable people do unreasonable things – and they don't take kindly to our attempts to stop them. The most effective way to deal with these people is to avoid them entirely. If you can't do that, then you may need some help. They use your emotions against you, which can make it hard to face them on your own.

Getting Started

1. Start with someone who's not likely to become aggressive when you stand your ground. This will give you the chance to become more comfortable setting boundaries.

2. Before approaching a person, notice what he or she says and does that you find difficult. What buttons are being pushed? Why are you saying *yes* when you'd rather say *no*? Understanding the dynamic will help you to choose a good response.

3. Start with statements about yourself, like "I'm busy today," "I need some time to think about this," or "I don't feel comfortable doing that." Continue with supportive statements

about the other person, such as, "I know you can handle it," or "I have faith in you."

4. Once you've decided what to say, you may want to practice a bit. Even though it's not real, it can help you to feel more comfortable when the time comes.

I hope you found these approaches easier than the more direct ones. Most situations can be handled diplomatically, and this chapter should give you plenty of ways to deal with them.

But sometimes the issue isn't your words. In fact, it isn't you at all. There are people who just won't take *no* for an answer, no matter how elegantly (or firmly) you say it. Our last tip will show you how to handle these stubborn folks without wasting valuable time trying to keep them happy.

Chapter 7

THE 7TH EASY WAY: THE BROKEN RECORD TECHNIQUE

The broken record technique can be used to reinforce any of the examples in this book. It's most appropriate when you've stated your decision clearly and someone is still trying to talk you out of it. If you don't take control of the conversation, you'll find yourself feeling angry and resentful – and running out of time for your other priorities.

This technique consists of repeating something over and over, until the other person finally figures out that you really mean it. It helps to use the same words, the same tone ... even the same look. The less variation, the more your part of the conversation resembles a broken record – and the more powerfully it makes your point.

The Formula

The formula is simple:

1. State your decision simply, clearly and firmly. Your words, your tone and the expression on

your face should all say the same thing: *Yes, I really mean it. No, it's not negotiable.*

2. Repeat as needed.

Here are some examples. Notice how boring and predictable the repetition is. Do it anyway; that's where the power lies.

I can't make it on Saturday. I already have plans. Next time, give me a few days' notice; I'd love to see everyone.

"But this will be way better than whatever you've got planned. Come with us. You won't regret it!"

I already have plans.

"But who knows when we'll get everyone together again. Do you know how long it took me to pull this off?"

I already have plans.

"You sound like a broken record! What do you have planned that's so fantastic?"

I already have plans. See you later.

It really is predictable, isn't it? That's just the point. Pretty soon the other person should be able to predict your response to any attempt to change your mind: *I already have plans.* And if he just doesn't get it – or refuses to take *no* for an answer – then it's time to move on. After all, how many times do you need to say it? Make sure that choice is yours, not someone

70

else's.

Let's look at another example. This one involves family:

> "I can't take Mom to her doctor's appointment tomorrow morning. Will you be a great sister and take her for me?"
>
> *I can't. I have an appointment of my own that I can't break.*
>
> "Can't you change it?"
>
> *I've already told you I can't.*
>
> "Please? I really need your help!"
>
> *I've already told you I can't.*

When the repetition gets to be too much, move on. This means leave the room, hang up the phone or close the subject and refuse to return to it. If you can't leave and someone tries to bring up the topic again, use the broken record technique again to set that boundary:

> "I know you said you can't, but won't you see what you can do about Mom's appointment tomorrow? I really need your help."
>
> *I've already told you I can't. I'm not discussing it any further.*
>
> "But I really need your help this time."
>
> *I'm not discussing it any further.*

[Fill in the continued attempts here....]

I'm not discussing it any further.

Yes, you will sound like a broken record. When the answer is *no*, you don't need to find ten different ways to say it. *No* is *no*. Nothing makes that point better than repetition.

Why isn't this easy for me?

You may find this approach difficult for a few reasons:

1. **You may find it hard to stand your ground when you're pushed.** If the original *no* takes courage, repeating it may take even more. And that's the whole point: someone is counting on you to give in to your fear.

2. **You may be sure of your decision but unsure of yourself.** This makes repeating yourself harder each time. In that case, it's better to end the conversation as quickly as possible.

3. **Repeating yourself may seem rude.** What's really rude, however, is to keep asking for something when the answer is clearly *no*. When someone keeps repeating the question, what's wrong with repeating the answer? If you're tired of repeating yourself, it's time to end the conversation.

Getting Started

1. **Express your decision firmly.** This means that your words, you tone of voice and the way you look at the person all indicate that

you mean it. This makes repetition super powerful.

2. **Take a deep breath and remember that it's OK to repeat yourself.** If your decision hasn't changed, why should anything else?

Decide how much repetition is enough. Once you've reached that point, refuse to discuss it again. Don't be held hostage by someone else's stubbornness.

Chapter 8

THE KEY TO
LASTING HAPPINESS

The best way to apply these "seven easy ways" in your life is to choose one and work with it. If you find yourself agreeing to things too quickly, go back to the first tip and practice buying yourself some time. Work with this until it becomes comfortable. Remember that you can decide whether to give a reason or let others know how you're feeling. What you choose to share depends on you and your relationships.

If you find yourself agreeing to things too quickly, go back to the first tip and practice buying yourself some time.

You may find that once you have the time to think clearly, many of your problems are easily solved. But if not, that's OK. That's what the other chapters are for.

Once you're comfortable taking the time you need, you're ready to consider the rest of the material. Don't try to do it all at once; choose the area that you relate to most, or to a situation that's important to you. Here's a summary to help you choose where to focus next:

Think outside the box. This is a great technique to use when you want to help, but you don't want to (or can't) do everything that's been asked of you. You can do this on your own, by telling others what you're willing to do for them. Or you can talk it through with them, sharing your needs and looking for a solution together. If limited time is your biggest problem (rather than people trying to manipulate you), this might be the place to focus.

Don't fall for charm and flattery. Do you have a hard time saying *no* to people who say that you're the only one who can help, or that they need you because you're so good at what you do? Or are you a sucker for charm, sacrificing things that matter to you in order to keep the good feelings coming? If so, then consider starting here. Pay special attention to how you feel in these situations. Often people who fall for flattery or charm are insecure about some aspect of themselves. If this is the case, you'll need to work on your sense of yourself. Are there some old wounds to heal? Once you're stronger and more confident, charm and flattery won't have the same effect.

Stop making excuses. Do you find yourself making excuses when you need to say *no*? If so, then this one is for you. Remember the difference between excuses and reasons: reasons are the truth, and we share them with people who have a right to know, or when we want someone to understand that we would help if we could. (This is how we remind others that we still care, even though we can't do what they've asked.) We make excuses when we're uncomfortable with the truth.

If you're comfortable buying time, look at how you're doing that. Are you making excuses for not agreeing to something right away? If so, then work on buying time without making excuses, perhaps starting with one person or one type of situation. Practice some of the more general responses, such as "Let me think about it and get back to you this afternoon." Notice what happens when you don't over-explain.

Once you can put off a decision without justifying yourself, you can move on to setting boundaries in the same way. Most people make excuses because they're afraid of rejection. Remind yourself – as often as needed – that if your boundary is reasonable, then rejection is not. People who reject you for setting a reasonable boundary aren't interested in your welfare, at least not in that moment. Their approval isn't worth chasing, particularly when the cost is your self-respect.

Handle manipulation directly. I reserve this approach for those people who can't take a hint or simply don't care about your needs. If you have someone like this in your life, you may find that this is your only option. If you found the suggestions in this chapter too difficult, consider starting with the polite approach to get some practice and become more comfortable. You may find that it works with some people, or at least in some situations. If that's not enough, then slowly move on to being more direct. Take baby steps and make sure you're comfortable before taking the next step. (Review the final paragraph on getting started for ideas.) It's important to give yourself the time you need to gain strength and confidence. Manipulators sense weakness, so focus on building yourself up rather than on getting an immediate result.

Handle manipulation politely. Not all manipulation needs to be confronted directly. If you know you're being manipulated, and you want to avoid a confrontation, then this a good place to focus. The approach here is to notice the form of the manipulation and politely refuse to give in to it. You might state that sometimes you need to put yourself first or that, in spite of feeling guilty, you won't change your mind. This lets people know that their tactics aren't working any more, but without you actually accusing them of anything. For many people, especially those who are usually reasonable, this is enough.

Become a broken record. Some people just won't take *no* for an answer. This technique lets them know that it's your only answer. If you're dealing with someone who doesn't respect your clearly stated boundaries, this could be the way to go. Once you've repeated yourself a few times (words, facial expression, tone of voice – the works!), walk away. A conversation is a two-way street, and it's up to you how long it lasts.

The key to using this book is to focus on one thing at a time and practice it until you feel comfortable. Start with whatever is most important right now. Reread that chapter. Think about anything that makes it harder for you and see if you can change that. Look at the tips for getting started and pick something that feels doable.

As circumstances change, you can always come back and choose another focus. Just take it one step at a time, and give yourself permission to try things out.

Remember that you have choices. Just as you can choose what information to share with whom, you can also choose whom to spend your time with and how often. If there are people in your life who consistently try to take advantage of you, then you may not want to be available the next time they call for lunch or coffee. As the saying goes, an ounce of prevention is worth a pound of cure.

I can tell you from personal experience that, even though it can be difficult, standing up for yourself is worth the effort. When you change an old pattern of pleasing everyone but yourself, you feel fantastic. Maybe it's because you've accomplished something really important. Or maybe it's simply because someone (you) is finally giving you the respect you deserve. You're the only one whose respect isn't optional.

Keep giving yourself that respect. You deserve it, and you're the only one who can be counted on to deliver it consistently. And if your recent choices don't seem worthy of respect, then I hope you'll respect yourself enough to make some changes.

That is my wish for you: that you insist on respecting yourself, regardless of how others treat you. Self-respect is always a choice. It is also one of the keys to lasting happiness.

WHAT'S NEXT?
A MESSAGE FROM
THE AUTHOR

If you've made it this far, I hope you've found what you were looking for: a simple guide to saying *no* when you need to.

But what if you want more?

Maybe you need to learn more. Or maybe you know what you need to do, but you just don't feel ready to do it. Setting boundaries can be scary – especially if you've been avoiding it for a while.

Don't worry; I've got you covered. Join my mailing list and I'll share more ideas about boundaries and relationships with you. You'll also be the first to know when I release a new book or course, offer a special deal on mentoring sessions or just publish a new article or video on my blog. And if you ever need to reach me, you'll know how.

Just go to **www.stephsterner.com** and join the party!

Or better yet, join my private Facebook group: Boundaries and Bridges. It's the place to be when you're struggling with just about any relationship. Join us and you can ask questions, exchange ideas, or give and receive support.

You can find us at **www.facebook.com/groups/ boundariesandbridges**.

Thanks for reading; I hope we can stay connected. And may your life be filled with people who respect both you and your boundaries.

Made in the USA
Lexington, KY
23 January 2018